Some [illegible]
Sermons

Some Windsor Sermons

The Rt Rev
Michael Mann

Dean of Windsor

MICHAEL RUSSELL

First published in Great Britain 1989
by Michael Russell (Publishing) Ltd,
The Chantry, Wilton, Salisbury, Wiltshire

Typeset in Sabon at The Spartan Press Ltd,
Lymington, Hampshire
Printed and bound in Great Britain
by Biddles Ltd, Guildford and King's Lynn

ISBN 0 85955 152 0

Contents

I
Abstinence

'GIVE US GRACE TO USE SUCH ABSTINENCE'

The Collect for the Second Sunday in Lent uses this word, 'abstinence', and it means 'doing without'. In these days that is not a popular concept. My daughter, when a schoolgirl at an Anglican convent school, was asked by one of the sisters, 'What are you giving up for Lent?' and she promptly replied 'Going to Chapel.' That was not a popular answer. In Britain today we do not believe in 'doing without'. The cry is for what I want, at once, without waiting or too much striving. What I want must be satisfied immediately my whim or fancy dictates.

As a boy I was taught to have a horror of debt. 'If you cannot pay for a thing, then you do without it.' Today we are positively encouraged to go into debt – hire purchase, credit facilities, easy terms; we live in a something-for-nothing era. Like Oliver Twist, all we can do is to hold out our begging bowl and cry for more and more. And the tragedy is that this attitude pervades every aspect of our personal and national life.

At the personal level a newly married couple expect their first home to be furnished in every respect at once. There is no question of saving, and gradually putting a home together; wall to wall carpeting, the most modern kitchen and so on, and all at once. There can be very few families that do not enter into debt in one way or another, and even our taxation system encourages you to take out a mortgage. At the corporate level, borrowing is a basic part of the system.

The Ibo people of Nigeria tell a story that in the beginning of the world there were only two human couples. They wandered the earth in search of water, which was very scarce in that heat. At last they came to a pool. One couple aggressively pushed the other two away, and jumped into the pool. They splashed about and washed themselves all over, drank their fill, and because they had plenty of water they washed away all their natural blackness and became white. When they had finished they allowed the second pair to enter the pool, but by that time there was only enough water left at the bottom of the pool for them to wet the soles of their feet and the palms of their hands. And that is why a black man has white palms to his hands and white soles to his feet.

The truth of this bitter tale lies in the way that others see us, in our aggressive, reckless, and selfish use of every precious thing on which we can lay our hands. Our Western profligate use of limited resources engenders a mental attitude that goes all too easily with a certain concept that has debased the once noble idea of the Welfare State. It says something like this. The world owes me a living. I expect everything to be done for me. I expect everything to be made easy. I expect my reward to be handed to me on a platter, in return for a constantly diminishing effort on my part.

Of course this is nothing new in human experience, or in history. Listen to the Prophets: Isaiah said (chapter 24, verses 1 and 2),

Beware the Lord will empty the earth,
Split it open and turn it upside down
And scatter its inhabitants.
Then it will be the same for priests and people,
Borrowers and lenders, debtor and creditor.

And Ezekiel had this to say (chapter 22, verse 12):

Men have accepted bribes to shed blood,
And they have executed discount and interest on their loans.
You have oppressed your fellows for gain,
And you have forgotten me.

The role of the prophet was not that of a foreteller, but of a *forth teller*. If you do this, and continue to behave in that way, then inevitably this will be the consequence. The reckoning may be put off in the short term, but you cannot avoid it in the long term; if you do not have to pay, your children will have to settle the account. If you turn from God, and from spiritual values, eventually you will inevitably destroy yourselves.

We need our prophets, even if they do make us feel uncomfortable, and indeed just because they do precisely that. This is particularly so nowadays, for the pressures are building up against our greedy, acquisitive form of Western civilisation. The dissatisfaction comes from both within and without. That sort of unlimited growth in which we are indulging cannot continue indefinitely. Pressures of population and our profligate use of non-renewable resources will bring us up against a variety of limits. There is never going to be enough of what we want for everyone. It is not only that there are not unlimited resources of oil, lead, copper and so on, for it can be argued that man's ingenuity will find alternatives to these material resources. In thirty years' time there will be double the number of people in the world that there are now. It took between 1800 and 1940 for the world's population to double, but as in all matters of compound interest, the doubling rate increases very rapidly, and it is now down to thirty years. This inevitably means that more people will be chasing ever-diminishing resources. But that is not all. We are discovering in Britain that we just do not have the ability or resources to do all the social things that technology has made possible and that we feel we ought to do, and that we want to do. There is just not enough to provide the high level of education, or of medical care, social security or defence, that we feel to be needed. There is a very real constraint upon the nation and particularly upon the Western world to think very hard about what ought to constitute 'good growth'.

One of our troubles is that we tend to think only in material terms. National growth has come to mean more of this or that thing, and above all else, more of it for *me*. This sort of attitude merely breeds the politics of greed and envy, and we see plenty of that.

In my Devonshire village during the last war, when there was a terrible shortage of meat, an elderly poacher made a great thing out of selling rabbit pies. One day a customer asked him, 'Where do you get all those rabbits?' On being pressed a bit harder the old man admitted that he mixed up the rabbit with a bit of horse meat – 'But I'm very fair, for I mixes it fifty fifty, one rabbit, one horse.' We still see too much of that sort of value today.

If we even think of abstinence, it is only in terms of doing without for a short time, in order that we may grab even more in the future. It is an extraordinary facet of modern thinking, and of our times, that no one seems prepared to stand still, but we must go on expanding until, like the proverbial balloon, we burst.

To the Christian, abstinence has a much more positive quality, and the Collect reminds us: 'Give us grace to *use* such abstinence.' The use of abstinence can bring out the best in us, and it can promote another dimension of human growth – that of the human spirit – for it can turn our minds away from our fascination with ourselves and with numbers, and direct our attention to quality rather than quantity.

There cannot be a parent who at some time or another has not had to face a decision in favour of abstinence and self-denial in order that their child may benefit. And such abstinence promotes spiritual growth, just because sacrifice is never wasted, and is never in vain. We all grow bigger by the unselfishness of doing without, in order that others may benefit and grow.

I often hear the comment concerning some sacrifice that, in human terms, seems to have been in vain; 'Oh, what a waste!' But abstinence and the sacrifice that results from it is never spiritually wasted, because it is an expression of love. Remember that Jesus told us that the greatest act of love that any one of us can make is to sacrifice our life for the benefit of someone else. He made that supreme act of love, 'Greater love hath no man than this, that he lay down his life for his friend.'

And this is not so altruistic as it may sound. My schooldays remind me of the fellow who died of a surfeit of lampreys. Perhaps that provides a warning for our condition. We need to diet, for our own spiritual good, for our own quality of life.

Abstinence, doing without, sacrifice, can be creative when we deny the material in order to nourish the spiritual. It is creative because it is concerned with love and grace and self-discipline, all of which help us to grow spiritually and to enhance the quality of our and others' lives.

'Give us grace to use such abstinence.'

2
Aids

'GO AND SIN NO MORE'

Recently a Bishop wrote to *The Times* on the subject of the new disease of Aids, and said that the Church of England is 'advocating chastity, not because we are moralising, but for practical prevention'. The Chairman of a Health Authority responded by saying that 'Moralising is a responsibility spiritual leaders should not avoid'. As the Bishop in question had been a Chairman of a Church Board, which has not been slow to moralise about unemployment, the inner cities, nuclear defence and other issues, I felt that I ought, even if it is only for my own peace of mind, to try to sort out what I feel might be a Christian response to this terrible new scourge that we have brought upon ourselves. So these are just my personal thoughts.

First of all, I have to look at the Bible. It seems to me that the Old Testament is very clear. As I understand it, Aids is contracted primarily through promiscuity, homosexuality, or drug abuse. Although drug abuse was not a factor in Old Testament times, promiscuity and homosexuality were very much of a problem. Leviticus (chapter 20, verse 13) states clearly: 'If a man lies with a male, both of them have committed an abomination, they shall be put to death.' Deuteronomy (chapter 23, verse 18) says: 'There shall be no prostitute of the daughters of Israel, neither shall there be a prostitute of the Sons of Israel. Both of these are an abomination to the Lord.' And again in Leviticus (chapter 20, verse 10) it states: 'If a man commits adultery, both shall be put to death.' The Old Testament seems to me pretty clear.

What about the New Testament? In the Gospels there is the story of the woman caught in the act of adultery, whom the Jews wanted to stone to death. Jesus' reaction was unequivocal; sternness mixed with compassion for human weakness – 'Neither do I condemn you', and he dismissed the women with 'Go and sin no more.' The Epistles are equally clear: 'Do not gratify the desires of the flesh, immorality, impurity, licentiousness.' (Galatians, chapter 5, verse 19.) And St Paul says again to the Romans (chapter 1, verse 26): 'Women exchanged natural relations for unnatural, and men likewise were consumed with passion for one another, receiving the due penalty for their errors.'

In spite of our 'permissive society' and attempts by some within the Church to be 'relevant', there is no getting around the fact that the Bible sees homosexuality as an abomination, and that both the Bible and the Christian Church have always taught that sexual relationships outside marriage are a sin. I think that needs to be stated clearly and categorically – for that is where I start from. As a Christian I cannot accept practising homosexual relationships as being natural, nor can I accept sexual permissiveness as being anything but a sin.

The Prophets of the Old Testament constantly warned the people of Israel about moral conduct: 'If you persist in doing this, then, inevitably, that will be the result.' There are some who might be tempted to say that the disease of Aids is God's judgement on a wicked world. I cannot see that, for my God is a God of Love, and not of retribution. Jesus did not say to the Jews: 'Go on and stone her'; he was certainly stern to the woman, 'Sin no more', but he was also compassionate, 'Neither do I condemn you.' To me the horror of sin is that it brings its own judgement, not that of God. Promiscuity and unnatural relationships will inevitably bring their own nemesis. But it is a judgement to which we condemn ourselves, and the punishment is that of our own making. If we persist in the unnatural, then we should not be surprised when Nature reacts against the unnatural.

But that is not the full horror of sin. If the results of sin were to be confined to those who committed the sin, we might feel that this was a stern but rough form of justice. But the terrible consequence of sin is that our sins so often involve the innocent. If we drive dangerously, it is someone else who is killed. The haemophilic child who contracts Aids through an infected blood transfusion suffers as the result of someone else's sin. As we get to know more about the disease, doubtless medical skill will try to protect the innocent and prevent infection; but knowledge comes from research, which is always dependent upon previous evidence. There is always a time lag. So the innocent will suffer.

We all have to take our share of responsibility for consenting to the moral state to which our society has sunk. Sexual relations between consenting adults of the same sex in private are legal, but that does not make them morally right. Efficient contraception makes sexual promiscuity easy and fashionable, but it is still sinful. As a result, all of us who have a vote have a shared responsibility. Parliament can only reflect what the nation feels and wants. Efficient contraception and changing social attitudes have removed a lot of previous fears and constraints. But because something is now possible does not necessarily make it right. Liberty can very easily degenerate into licence, particularly when restraint and self-discipline become unfashionable. Our trouble is that very few people see anything wrong in this behaviour, and indeed, even within the Church, scorn is poured upon those who defend traditional values, and they are castigated as being old-fashioned and out of touch. If Aids is Nature's means of redressing that balance, it may be, sadly, at a terrible cost.

Politicians, rightly, are concentrating on a massive campaign of prevention by warning, and by advocating precautionary measures. But this is like the lesson to be learnt from the Parable of the Good Samaritan. Yes, as Christians, of course we must do our utmost to bind up the wounds of those who are hurt, and to care for them with compassion. But first aid and compassion are not enough. In the case of the Good Samaritan, if they had got rid of the robbers, there would have been no need to pick anyone out of the ditch. Prevention has to be accompanied by cure, and not only cure of the disease itself, important as that may be; we need to cure the moral state that enables this to happen, and the only cure for sin is repentance.

This is just what is lacking, a sense of what is right and wrong. In all that we hear about this terrible new scourge, there is no note of guilt or sorrow. Rather the attitude seems to be: 'One day we shall find a cure, and then we can go on as before, without any sense of fear.' That is a fool's paradise. The moral lesson of Aids is that sin always brings its own retribution in one way or another. I believe that Christians need to stand up and be counted in today's society. That means that we have got to be prepared to say out loud and clear that permissiveness has gone too far; that homosexuality and promiscuity are wrong; and that until our society – and that means *you* and *me* – recognises this, we shall continue bringing upon ourselves disaster and scourges such as Aids. Then all that is left to us is compassion for the suffering. Jesus showed that compassion, and so must we, but remember Jesus also said: 'Go and sin no more.'

3
Cancer

'LOVE GOD, AND LOVE YOUR NEIGHBOUR'

Jesus used to put over the point he wanted to make by taking an example with which everyone was familiar, and saying, 'Look at that man sowing corn on the hillside there,' or, 'A friend of mine was giving a party the other day,' or, 'Someone I know owned a vineyard.' These were instances which were the commonplace experiences of everyday life, but which in each case helped people to see with two pairs of eyes; with the one, the material world in which we are all immersed, but also, with the other, the spiritual world, which lies within and behind that material experience.

When I was a boy at preparatory school, my mother came to see me to tell me that she had cancer. Fourteen years later, after a great deal of suffering and many operations, all of which she rose above with an unconquerable spirit, with tremendous courage and wonderful humour, the disease finally won over her physical body, but never over her spirit. I suppose that fourteen years of battle taught me and my brothers more about the spiritual side of life than if our mother had died of a hearty old age.

Today, because of the results of scientific research, we know much more about cancer. What we know is still not enough, but it is more than we knew then, and no case today seems as hopeless as it used to be. We know some of the causes, such as smoking, inhaling particles of asbestos, being subject to doses of radiation, psychological stress and strain. And we now have eyes that spot the first signs so much earlier. What we do know is that the word 'cancer' covers a whole family of diseases, all of which originate in some malfunctioning of the cells of our body.

There are parts of our body which wear out continually, and have to be replaced by the natural functioning of the system; this is done by the cells of our body splitting, so creating new cells which can replace the old and worn out ones. This process, which is going on all the time, requires that each molecule, or cell, splits so that the new cell is an exact replica of the old. The nucleus of each cell contains a substance which is called DNA, and this is important, because it is like a computer code, which gives the new cell all the right information about our particular make-up and needs, and so enables it to be reproduced exactly without any error.

But sometimes this split can go wrong, and the DNA does not transmit its information, and then the new cell's relationship with its neighbours breaks down, so that its activity is no longer in harmony with those of its neighbours or of the whole body. As a result it becomes isolated, and as it, in its turn, starts to split and reproduce, it breeds other cells like itself out of tune with the healthy cells. These rogue cells then form a growth, or cancer, which, if unchecked, can eventually take over from the healthy body.

These facts have been discovered as a result of scientific research. And it is that very research which seems so often to dazzle the eyes of many people, leading them to think that religion is out of date, merely a throwback to a less sophisticated age and a primitive attempt to explain the mysteries which science, given the time, will make perfectly and logically clear. And yet scientists themselves are beginning to see a spiritual meaning behind the knowledge which they acquire.

Many scientists see this sort of research as typical of the methods adopted by Jesus, in that it can provide a parable about human relationships, and about modern living. It is odd that respect for the results of scientific research, which among ordinary people is so very great, should yet be viewed only with material eyes for the actual quantifiable physical results, when there is also a spiritual aspect to be discerned. We seem to have gone overboard in our insistence on the importance of the individual – and he is important – but that importance has to be balanced against the needs of others. We lay stress on individuality – on self-fulfilment, self-gratification, self-understanding – but the danger in all this is that we forget others. A man commits a crime and we explain it away that it is because he is psychologically maladjusted, or his mother dropped him as a child. A marriage goes onto the rocks and it is because the couple are incompatible. We have tried to become so independent that if we look at the spiritual lessons to be learnt from medical research we may see that we are becoming like those rogue cells, which then form a spiritual cancer. And if we take the time to think about it, we do know that it is a cancer. Independence taken to its logical conclusion is not only impossible, it results in that most terrible of all spiritual maladies, loneliness. We need others for a healthy life, and indeed we can only be healthy in relation to others.

When we behave aggressively, in a manner that takes no account of others or which refuses to be constrained by our relationships with our neighbours, then the spiritual cancer of 'self' and an attitude of 'I couldn't care less' takes over, and that soon produces symptoms of a spiritual cancer – vandalism, football hooliganism, drugs, violence – and all the worst attributes of contemporary society.

We all cherish our independence, yet not one of us can live without other people, for we are all dependent upon each other. That is why Jesus told us that there are only two things that really matter – to love God, and to love our neighbour as ourself. When we love ourselves to an inordinate extent, then we forget to love our neighbour, and then the inordinate chokes co-ordination.

If physical cancer is the lawless and rogue element related to the requirements of the body, there is also a spiritual cancer which is just as capable of destroying the health of our society. Physical cancer has to be dealt with at an early stage, and the treatment, to be successful, often has to be drastic. When we live only to ourselves, and become absorbed with selfish things, our relationships with others do then come under strain, and start to break down. That spiritual cancer, unchecked, will surely result in a spiritual growth of selfishness and extreme independence which offends the whole body, just because it disregards the laws of human conduct. In the final state that will be as fatally terminal to our health as a people as its physical counterpart.

Perhaps we need to take to heart the lessons which scientific research affords us, and to look at it with eyes that comprehend not only the material results of that research, but also the spiritual truths which it underlines.

'Love God, and love your neighbour.'

4
Christmas Day

We live in a nervous and anxious world, a world where peace and goodwill among men ultimately depends upon the confidence and trust each of us can have in one another. So long as any society is stable and ordered, people are able to live their lives with a fair degree of certainty. They know what is expected of them and, within that assurance, there is room to be tolerant of other ways and habits. But there sometimes comes a period when the old ways no longer seem to satisfy, and we lose that sense of security and stability. The birth of Jesus came during such a period.

The Jews were uneasy under the centralised Roman rule which brought an alien Latin law, which seemed to ignore local differences and needs. Thinking Jews were questioning the rigid institutionalised system of their own religious observance. Certainly it gave them a sense of national identity, but it also caused frustration in that it no longer seemed to speak to their spiritual needs. The old ways no longer possessed their former authority and too many people were looking for something new.

The Romans could sense this feeling of unrest and were ready to respond with military severity; Herod was frightened by it and, like all frightened people, over-reacted; the Wise Men were sensitive to new signs and went to great trouble to explore any possibility; the shepherds, confronted with something which they did not understand, were curious: 'Let us go and see this thing.' For when we live in a period of uncertainty, we all have a choice. We can face the future with hope or with fear.

We all have to come to terms with uncertainty. Even though knowledge has increased enormously, there will always be important elements of uncertainty in human existence. It is so easy for uncertainty to breed fear, unless we have a base line of faith, which is able to see the good in the present and gives us hope for the future.

Until recently, for many, science seemed able to provide that faith. The incredible advances of this century reinforced the sense of secular confidence, and still do for many people. But others, and particularly scientists, were not so sure. It seems that the more we learn, the more we discover how much there is yet to know. And no matter how carefully we test our discoveries, their application too often produces unforeseen and harmful results. In 1927 the physicist Heisenberg showed that every scientific description contains some essential uncertainty; a threatening proposition for those who want the assurance of a mechanistic creation which always obeys its own rules. But the mark of the scientist is that of humble enquiry, resulting in awe at what unfolds before his eyes.

The one thing that the Wise Men seemed wise enough to understand was that that the outward assurance of Herod ('Come back and tell me all about it') was based on an arrogance and a fear that boded no good. We need to be careful of those who offer conviction without qualification, and who exclude the possibility of doubt. If you know that you are right, then everyone else must be wrong or misguided. That sort of certainty is a small step from the arrogance that breeds intolerance.

Uncertainty about the present, and fear for the future, can bring about a loss of nerve for those who reject authoritarian answers. Too many Christians seem to have lost confidence, and become infected with a negative attitude. A lack of faith leads to a profound pessimism, which sees everything as worse than it used to be. And the media encourage pessimism by their fascination with the sensational.

When we try to anticipate calamity we so often over-react, like Herod, because the actual is seldom as bad as our forebodings led us to anticipate. One of God's greatest gifts to mankind is to deny us knowledge of the future. Total knowledge would be a burden too terrible to be borne.

But faith is much more than the acceptance of uncertainty. A few feet from where I stand lie the mortal remains of His late Majesty King George VI. Above them is inscribed those words that he used at that first Christmas broadcast of the war in 1939: 'I said to the man who stood at the gate of the year, "Give me a light that I may tread safely into the unknown." And he replied, "Go out into the darkness and put your hand into the hand of God. That shall be to you better than a light and safer than a known way." '

Faith enables us to live with uncertainty because we are able to trust in the goodness of God, as we step out into the darkness of the future. But it is to God that we need to look, not to our fellow men, whose failings and imperfections so often seem to come between us and our vision of God.

Faith involves trusting people, yes, but people will go on letting us down, be they bishops, politicians or businessmen, because people are mortal and human. We can only go on trusting people because we have the ultimate faith in something that is not passing but eternal. When others fail us, it is their human frailty, like our own, that lets us down, but it is a frailty that we are able to set against the unchanging and constant love of God.

Jesus had no comfort of certainty from the moment of his birth –not even a bed in which to be born – nor in the those first few weeks of life, as they fled from Herod, the physical assurance of the safety which a family home affords. But even as a boy he had a spiritual assurance, a closeness to God, that gave hope or wonder to all who met him, as it still does today.

The acceptance of the uncertainties of life involves faith: a faith that is not blind credulity, but that helps us to accept in awe, yet with hope those things we do not understand, because we have a basic confidence in the ultimate purpose of our life within the whole of God's Creation. Uncertainty seems to be part of God's design, perhaps to keep us humble and remind us that we are human, but Christians can accept the unknowable with peace of mind through the assurance of faith in the purpose of our journey and the unchanging love of God to support and to sustain us.

Those shepherds and Wise Men, confronted with the manger and its precious burden, knelt down and worshipped. We need to recover our confidence, lift up our eyes and join them in faith and with renewed hope in front of this Holy Child.

Go out into the darkness of our world and, in the midst of all your uncertainties, put your hand into the hand of God. 'That shall be better to you than a light, and safer than a known way.'

5
The Church

Last year was not a good year for the Church of England. A leader in a major national newspaper said: 'The Church of England must redeem the honour it has allowed so foolishly, publicly and tragically to be tarnished.' If we feel unable to ally ourselves to such harsh sentiments, expressed as unkindly as members of the Church of England have grown to expect from some sections of the media, many of us do probably feel a sense of bewilderment at the way in which the Church seems to have been behaving over the past year, and before.

People look to the Church for a number of reasons, and some will place more emphasis on one aspect and some on another. But in broad terms the Church is there to bring men and women to God, and God to men and women, through the Sacraments, through the word of God as revealed in the Scriptures, and through prayer. To give a very general description, this pointing to God is achieved on both a personal and individual level, as well as on a communal basis, through the worship and ministrations of the Church.

But the lay people of the Church of England have come to expect more than this, and it is a great compliment to the past services of the parochial clergy that this should be so. Over the past forty difficult years nothing has upset people more than to have their parish priest removed, or to be made to join up and share his services with others. They may not have liked Mr so and so, or think that the vicar doesn't do this or should do more of that, but overall, even to those with a minimal contact with the Church, the presence of a parson in their midst has been seen as an asset and something to be valued.

In a time of change we all need our bench-marks, our points of reference to which to turn so that we are able to keep our heads whilst all around are losing theirs. Change is nothing new, for we are all changing all the time, but the social change which we are facing is surely somewhat different. Forty years ago change meant progress. We were changing things so that they would be better and fairer, and in order to do this there needed to be more of everything – more education, more houses, more medical care, more television, more jobs. A young person learnt a trade or profession and could then expect that to be his career for life: no one could say that to a young school leaver today with any confidence. Whole industrial skills and professions have changed out of all recognition, and many have disappeared. We seem to have too many cars and too many people. It is this sense of uncertainty, of not being sure any longer where it is that we are heading, that makes the basic continuities of life even more important than before. For instance, I am sure that one major reason for the absorbing interest that is shown in the Royal Family is that, in people's minds, they stand for good example, stability, sanity and assurance in the quicksands of contemporary life. Many people feel that the Church ought to provide the same assurance.

I am convinced that the succession of unhappy events in the life of the Church over the past year merely shows that this hope is an illusion. And it is an illusion because it is based upon a false hope. We have directed our gaze in the wrong direction, and we have allowed ourselves to become mesmerised by the influences of this wicked world; we have become obsessed with the doings – and mostly the scandalous doings – of our fellow human beings. We have developed a false image of the Church, and we have placed upon it expectations that it can never fulfil, because those expectations are based upon the values of our society, and too many of those values are corrupt.

Everyone of us who is a Christian believes that we have this in common, that each of us will have to render an account to God of the way in which we have lived our lives. The teachings of Jesus are full of these warnings – the Parable of the Talents, the Parable of the Vineyard, 'Whoever offends one of these little ones, it were better for him that a millstone should be hung around his neck, and he be cast into the sea'; if your eye or your foot offends you, it is better to pluck it out or cut it off, than thus to enter the Kingdom of Heaven. The theme of judgement and of personal responsibility runs continuously and powerfully through the teaching of Jesus.

When *you* stand before the judgement seat of God, and you are asked, 'Why did you do this?' or 'Why did you not do that?', what sort of answer will it be to say 'Oh, I was put off by the Bishop of X', or 'Oh, I gave up on God because the General Synod was so unsatisfactory', or just, 'I didn't like my parson'? Or even more likely, 'I was too busy'.

We are becoming so bemused with what is being dangled in front of our eyes concerning the sensational shortcomings and inadequacies of our fellow creatures that we no longer look beyond them to the things that are eternal. You will know that lovely Collect from the Book of Common Prayer, 'Grant, Lord, that we may so pass through things temporal, that we finally lose not the things eternal': but that is what is happening, we are losing sight of the things eternal.

The failure of the Church has not been in its human scandals, shortcomings or inadequacies, it has been in that it has itself become so preoccupied with the politics of the here and now. As a result it has failed to lift up *your* eyes both to the spiritual present and to the hereafter: as the Prayer Book puts it, 'to the means of grace, and to the hope of glory'.

If you fix your eyes on your fellow humans, be they archbishop, dean, canon, parish priest or fellow Christian, you will be disappointed, for all the world is odd, except thee and me, and even thee's a bit off!

The Church *is* still a bulwark, and a rock of assurance in an age of discontinuity. But it is not a bastion because of its clergy or its officers, but because of God, and because it offers the means of grace in this life through the Sacraments of God, through the teaching of the Bible, and through the discipline of prayer and meditation. It is through this grace that we poor humans, in all our frailty, are enabled to rise above our mean, petty and selfish natures, and have the power of the Holy Spirit to bring comfort and succour to our neighbour, whoever that may be. And we do this out of love of God, and in the hope that when we have to answer for our lives, God may have mercy on our shortcomings, and grant us that share of glory, for which Jesus Christ suffered, died and rose again for *you* and *me*.

6
Death

'I SAW A NEW HEAVEN'

I suppose that giant telescopes, black holes in outer space, and the wonders of space travel with men walking on the moon have destroyed the rather naive and childish picture, which has nourished Christians for centuries, of a belief of a Heaven up there above the clouds.

Indeed, in our daily lives we do not need hymns like 'Up above the Sky He's King' to remind us that the very word Heaven directs our thoughts to the sky – 'Heavens above!' When we speak of 'The Heavens', we automatically think of stars, planets and constellations. This image is so firmly fixed in our minds that we find it very difficult not to think of God as an old man 'up there', and if that is where he abides, then 'Heaven' must be 'up there' with him. Yet as we learn of the incredible vastness of space, with galaxies of planets, and stars millions and millions of light years away, it does seem to reinforce the uneasy feeling that religion has been proved to be nothing more than a childish need of earlier and more trusting generations. We, the enlightened, should surely have no further need for such myths – good heavens, no!

But John in his revelation saw a *new* Heaven. That is what we need. And we need it for two reasons: the first is for our comfort, and the second is for our discomfort.

One of the reasons why the Christian faith seems to have so little hold on the common imagination is that the world has become absorbed in things material. All that seems to matter is what happens in *this* world. We have become infatuated with the things of today, and tomorrow is too often left to look after itself. Yet the one certain fact of life is death. None of us, old or young, rich or poor, queen or commoner, can avoid the certainty that everyone of us will die. We prefer not to dwell on this uncomfortable fact. It is thought of as morbid or tactless; death has become an unmentionable subject. It is quite extraordinary that in such a practical and materialistic age such an inevitable fact should be so sedulously avoided. We pride ourselves upon facing up to facts, and yet we deliberately try to shut our eyes to the one great fact of life – its termination. For if you have not faced up to the fact of your impending death, you have not started to face up to life.

The Christian faith means nothing if it does not provide the answer to that great fact. Jesus Christ was not just a saintly person, a wise and very good man. He was executed, and died, as you and I must do one day. But the Christian believes that Jesus conquered death and rose from his grave. As St Paul pointed out, we are of all people the most wretched if we do not believe this. And Jesus promised that where he goes, we shall follow. Without a belief in life after death we are indeed without hope and hopeless.

What sort of existence is Christianity offering when it speaks of life eternal? We know very little – all that we have been given are a few signposts, and the first points towards what Heaven is not. Jesus, in answer to a trick question from the Sadducees about a woman who, through death, became the wife to a whole series of brothers, pointed out that in the afterlife there is no giving and taking in marriage. It is a spiritual existence, rather than a material one.

St Paul helps us with an analogy. In writing to the Corinthians, he compares life after death to the difference between a seed and the full grown plant. The shape and feel of the seed is completely different from that of the mature plant, be it wheat or a flower. So life after death is beyond our imagination because it will be so different. 'So it is with the resurrection of the dead. What is sown perishable, is raised imperishable. It is sown a physical body, it is raised a spiritual body.'

What we do know is that it was the fact of the Resurrection that spread Christianity all over the world. 'We would not have you ignorant, brethren, concerning those who are asleep, that you may not grieve as others do who have no hope.' And Peter says, 'Praise be to the God and Father of Our Lord Jesus Christ who in

His great mercy gave us new birth unto a living hope by the Resurrection of Jesus Christ from the dead.' Jesus himself told us, 'If a man has faith in me, even though he die, he shall come to life, and no one who is alive and has faith in me shall ever die.'

As a priest it had often been my privilege to sit by the dying. In my experience there sometimes comes a period near to death when the dying person is half in this world and half beyond it. I remember an old lady, who had been in a semi-coma, suddenly clasping my hand, and saying, 'Can't you see them? Can't you see them? They are so lovely.' And then she died. This sort of experience is not uncommon with the dying, and it is as if they are partly in this world and partly in a world we can neither see nor enter, and which we are not allowed to experience.

I have lost a number of people whom I have loved very dearly, and this is an enormous comfort to me. Life would be very cruel and purposeless if I had no hope – if I sincerely believed that life just snuffs out, and that is the end of it. A Scottish theologian, John Baillie, put it this way: 'We are faced with two alternatives, on the one hand a radical pessimism and on the other the hope of everlasting life. The pessimist deserves to be honoured with our most deep and sympathetic, and even affectionate understanding. It is a dark night of the soul at which none of us can afford to sneer, remembering that if we have passed into the brightness of the Christian expectation, the praise is not to us, but to the grace of God in Our Lord Jesus Christ.'

But there is also a discomforting side. We are told quite bluntly that Heaven is not necessarily guaranteed. It will matter how you have lived this life. The sheep will be separated from the goats. It is probably rather unfashionable to think in terms of crime and punishment in these days when every possible psychological excuse is proffered for bad behaviour. But in thinking of a *new* Heaven, whatever that future existence of the human spirit may hold for us beyond the grave, we shall be deluding ourselves if we do not take to heart the stern and unequivocal warnings that so often seem to get glossed over. It does matter how you live, it does matter what you say, it does matter how you treat others. And, however it may work out, we are told that the quality of that future existence after death does depend upon the quality of our life here on earth.

Perhaps we all need to see a 'new Heaven'.

7
Good Friday

As I walk around St George's Chapel, or show visitors its timeless beauty, one thing constantly strikes me. The present Chapel was built between 1475 and 1490, and the men and women of that era had an obsession with death: not so much with the act of dying, but with what would happen to their souls after they had died.

In what is, after all, a fairly small collegiate church, there are nine medieval chantry chapels. A chantry chapel was built so that a priest might pray daily for the soul of the departed. It involved not only the building of the chapel itself, often a very elaborate affair, but also the permanent endowment for the provision of a priest to offer the daily prayers.

Those men and women were very conscious of their own mortality, and of their own human sinfulness and weakness. They knew that they had to answer for the way in which they had lived, and most of them, then as now, had a good deal for which to answer – kings, lord chancellors, deans, noblemen and canons. And they knew that their only hope lay in Jesus. Jesus, who on this day, suffered not for his own wrongdoings, but for theirs and ours.

What a change has come over people today! The word 'sin' is out of date and holds little power. We no longer commit sin; we are psychologically disturbed, or emotionally upset, or the mind is unbalanced, or perhaps, in an age of reason, we are just irrational. And yet one would think that the events of the past fifty years have offered as much evidence of sheer wickedness and evil as any other epoch.

What has happened? Perhaps one cause may be that the suffering and death of Jesus, let alone his resurrection, no longer means very much to most of us. We can see others' faults only too clearly, but our own are usually excusable and are never – well, hardly ever – bad enough to haunt us with guilt or the need for forgiveness.

And yet from time to time in our lives, events do suddenly face us which cause us to regret bitterly what we have done, or, more often, with what we have left undone. And it is at times like these – on today, Good Friday – that we catch a glimpse of the horror of sin and of our human need for forgiveness and absolution.

For the men of 1490, the burden of guilt for their sins was unbearable, and, indeed, it remains so today for those who actually realise their guilt, and who frequently end up, as a result, in mental homes or with a breakdown. But the men of 1490 knew that there was another way of escape from their sense of inadequacy and guilt. It was, and still is, in turning to God and asking for, and receiving, forgiveness.

For most of us, sin does not mean murder or grievous bodily harm. It is probably unlikely even to be deliberate. It is much more likely to be thoughtlessness, selfishness, arrogance, greed or sheer temper. The terrible thing is that it never just affects us; it always damages or hurts someone, or something, else. This is true of even such a simple thing as the effect we have on others; it is so easy by commission or omission to inflict hurt, because each one of us is so sensitive. And those who are hurt may readily forgive, but it takes much longer to forget.

On the Cross on this Good Friday we see something of the depth of Jesus' compassion, for his executioners, for the thief beside him, for his mother; and all this in spite of his own agony. He asked forgiveness for the rough Roman soldiers because they did not know what they were doing. We, like the penitent thief, *do* know what we do; and without that sense of wrongdoing there is no forgiveness. But with penitence comes all the compassion and healing power of forgiveness, and not only forgiveness but new life. We need to find out afresh that this is why Jesus died for you and me on this Good Friday.

8
Easter Day

It is extraordinary how many Christians in the West seem to have ceased to believe in the Easter message, and have trivialised this festival down to chocolate eggs, congestion at the Channel ports, and a new outfit. I suppose that this loss of belief started with the Renaissance, and came to its fulfilment with man's pride in the wonders of science and technology. Leading politicians seem to see the Christian faith merely as the guardian of morality. Church leaders come over on television as confused and defensive. Even Hans Kung, one of our greatest living theologians, sees the Resurrection as 'nothing more than the satisfaction of man's longing for his personal immortality'.

Kant in *The Critique of Pure Reason* posed three questions: 'What can I know?'; 'What ought I to do?'; and, 'What may I hope for?' These three questions point out the three differing facets of human reason. 'What can I know?' illustrates the logical aspect of the mind; we search for clues, put together the data, and then assess what we have gathered. 'What ought I to do?' emphasises the practical side of reason: we evaluate the facts, and by a process of intuition we come to a decision. That is why it is often said that women are more practical than men, for they often have a more highly developed sense of intuition. 'What may I hope for?' points to the creative aspect of reason, where imagination helps us to act inventively with new insights.

What can we know about Easter? We know that the disciples believed that they had seen the Risen Christ. As St Augustine put it: 'It is incredible that men so rude and lowly, so few and unaccomplished, should have convinced the world, including men of learning, of something so incredible.' The Buddha, Confucius and Mahomet all lived long lives, teaching their disciples for many years and ending their lives in honour. Jesus' public career was very brief, and it ended in a shameful and humiliating manner. And Christians did not preach Jesus as yet another martyr-prophet, like John the Baptist, but, incredibly, as risen from the dead. Those early disciples, and the eleven Apostles, were convinced that they themselves had seen and heard and touched the Risen Lord. Of course we can rule out the possibility of the Resurrection on the grounds that it is contrary to the laws of nature. But to do that would be to show a closed mind, and most scientists today would reject such a determinist bias, for we are rediscovering that the laws of nature are even more complex than we thought.

These then are the facts that we know about Easter. Perhaps we have taught too much about Jesus' life and preaching, and not enough about his death and resurrection. We have concentrated upon the Incarnation at the expense of the Resurrection. So what ought we to do? We know that the grace of God is a free gift, and that we often meet it where we least expect it. There is, however, still the need for a personal response. We can never eliminate the element of risk which faith in the Resurrection always involves. It is not just the acceptance of historical evidence, for that would be to confine the Resurrection to the laws of evidence; it is because God in this amazing event has gone outside those boundaries that it requires a decision of faith.

We need to remember that with the preaching of the Resurrection came also the warning of judgement. As Paul wrote to the Romans, those who accept the 'good news' of Christ's victory over death are meant now to be 'dead unto sin and alive unto God'. The Resurrection is not only about the promise of a life hereafter, it is to be open to the power and grace of the Risen Lord to overcome our many trials and weaknesses in this world – here and now.

The evidence from the Epistles and the early Church is full of the promise together with the warning. Peter praises 'the God and Father of our Lord Jesus Christ, who in his great mercy gave us new birth into a living hope by the resurrection of Jesus Christ from the dead'. And Paul points out to the Corinthians that there is no hope for those who, having accepted Christ, then behave disgracefully. Peter at Pentecost preached to the Jews: 'Repent and be baptised.' Repentance turns us away from ourselves and leads us to have compassion for others – for those who suffer – and to a longing for justice, following the example of Jesus himself set by his many acts of healing, and in his condemnation of the behaviour of the scribes and Pharisees; and in his praise, for instance, of Zaccheus, when that tax-collector resolved to restore what he had cheated from others.

We have to balance the contradiction of the pain of the Cross with the surprise and joy of the Resurrection. It is a balance between human freedom and divine grace. Unfortunately we seem to have blunted our sense of sin, and made everything subject to excuse and explanation. As a result human freedom is so often used in a negative manner, destroying the very relationships and the creation, which God has entrusted to our care. And if we are not careful, we shall destroy ourselves.

So what ought we to do? That has always been clear – repent. What an unfashionable word, and how we dislike saying 'I was wrong, I am sorry'. The Easter message is to be 'dead unto sin, and alive unto righteousness'.

That brings us to Kant's third question: 'What may I hope for?' Belief in the Resurrection confers both the grace to be forgiven one's sins in this life, and the hope of eternal life after death. We are called to a faith in the future of this world, and to belief in the promise of Life Eternal. So it is from that perspective that we are called to live our lives now – as trustees here for a brief moment of time, but as part of the Communion of Saints beyond this life.

We shall only rediscover the rightness of life when we regain a wider vision – the balance between logic, intuition and imagination. We know a great deal, but the question 'What can I know?' implies that knowledge itself is neutral, and what matters is the use to which we put our knowledge. Logic must be tempered with intuition and imagination. 'What ought I to do?' requires us to seek the grace to enable us to act with vision, because we have this Easter hope for the future. It is a future that has within it concern and compassion for this world – for God's creation – and also for a personal future for you and me that is no longer limited to our brief human span, but encompasses the promise, through this Resurrection, of a life after death within the glory of God, and in the company of those who have gone before us. Easter is the central core of the Christian faith. Its proclamation is at the heart of any recovery of faith and of the will to act responsibly, for we embrace the stuff of eternity and we are called to live our lives in the light of an eternal destiny.

9
Dominion

'AND GOD SAID, "BE FRUITFUL AND MULTIPLY, AND FILL THE EARTH AND SUBDUE IT; AND HAVE DOMINION OVER EVERY LIVING THING."'
GENESIS, CHAPTER 1, VERSE 28

In spite of many doubts about the literal truth of the Genesis story, that command for man to have dominion over the world has been accepted by Christians, Muslims and Jews without question. We seem to believe that the world exists for man and for man alone. If that is so, does not man have a duty to act responsibly in discharge of that trust placed in him by God?

When the Bible was written, man's need to propagate and to increase was not a problem, for the world was under-peopled. Today we face a different situation. In the last two centuries the population of the world has quadrupled, but like all compound interest, the doubling time is constantly shortening, and is now down to only thirty years. More people occupy more space and make greater demands on natural resources. When I went to Nigeria in 1946, the population of that African country was estimated to be 27 million people: today that estimate has risen to 100 million, and the standard of living, in spite of their oil wealth, has hardly improved. In poorer countries there has been a decline.

Genesis tells us to subdue the earth, but the demands of increasing population mean that we are stripping it in order to satisfy the basic needs of that population. And we are doing it so ruthlessly that many vital resources are being used up faster than they can be renewed, and many others are not renewable. This short-sighted exploitation is also upsetting the balance of nature, with long-term effects which could be disastrous. This was not a problem the people of early Bible times had to face. The situation is sufficiently serious that, within the lifetime of our choristers, irreparable and irreversible damage will have been done to the very earth on which we depend for our existence. Yet there is no general sense of urgency, or even of moral obligation. We do not seem to be aware of the rights and wrongs of the situation. There is a growing unease, especially among the young and some intellectuals, which is evidenced by the growth of 'Green' parties and environmental lobbies. But much of that unease is confused, more of it is based on sentiment or radical protest; and so it tends to be dismissed.

If an animal is maltreated or hunted, there is an immediate sentimental outcry. When man so mismanages his affairs that a nuclear disaster occurs or a major river is polluted for miles, the effects are shrugged off. There is hardly the same sense of outrage as when a cat is maltreated. We are so deeply imbued with the knowledge that man is supreme that even though accidents do happen due solely to human frailty, there appears to be no deep moral feeling of wrong. For how much longer can we accept that man has an unlimited biblical authority to exploit? And in so far as he does, should he continue to do so selfishly, and only for human ends, and with little thought for the future?

Victorian Christianity was driven by an urge to civilise the world; 'O'er heathen lands afar, thick darkness broodeth yet.' But this was a civilising urge that was based upon trade and the making of money, which has reached its fulfilment in modern Western materialism. Our ingenuity and skill has lengthened human life, reduced mortality and offered a minority a very high material standard of living. But by so doing we have raised even deeper moral questions about the future of the world on which we depend, and the manner in which we treat it.

Western materialism has been linked with greed, and when this happens, envy is never far behind. The leading so-called Christian countries have achieved standards which cannot be realised by the whole of mankind. This is bound to create envy and resentment among the 'have-nots', as we are now beginning to see. And are we really so convinced as Christians that our Western style of materialism is a Christian way of life? Have our standards been helpful to the Aborigines of Australia, the Red Indians of North America or the Eskimos of Canada? Does our greediness really suit so-called primitive cultures and peoples? So often these people seem to absorb all the worst aspects of our civilisation and are unable to adapt to the good.

Western-style democracy presents a second danger when it is allied to commercial materialism. One of the weaknesses of democracy is that it concentrates attention on the short-term expediency, too often at the expense of long-term vitality. Concentration on the present reinforces greed and envy, as we look over our shoulders to see what others are doing or getting. But when we start to think about how a Christian should interpret his dominion over nature, we are thinking in terms of trusteeship, and, therefore, in terms of the future, and often the long-term future.

In Thackeray's story 'The Rose and the Ring', the good Fairy Godmother Blackstick's birthday present to the Prince and Princess was a little misfortune, in order to toughen them up and equip them for reality. Surely we ought not to allow crisis to be the only spur for the action which we should have taken long ago? Does not the Christian faith have something to say about what you and I ought to believe?

In the first place man's own survival is at stake. But powerful as that reason is, I do not think it is enough for the Christian, because it is basically a selfish reason.

We are commanded to love God, and our neighbour. This golden rule rightly focuses our attention upon other human beings. Man's dominion over God's creation is a trust, and trusteeship demands respect for that which is under trust. If this is God's world, it demands respect because it is God's. Nature has its own intrinsic moral standing, and claims of obligation.

Some will say that nature itself is cruel, 'red in tooth and claw'. Nature is dynamic, and interference with that dynamism upsets a whole balance of delicately interlocking forces. But if this is God's world, then surely it is man's moral duty to respect the way in which it functions. Too often we blindly crash in for our own selfish ends, as in the destruction of the tropical rain forest, without pausing to think of the effects that our activity will have in that case on the climate or on the eighty per cent of all known species of both plants and animals that are dependent on the forest. Even when we start out with the best intentions, we cannot always foresee the results. We are only just starting to understand how all life on earth, in the oceans and in the atmosphere is interconnected, and that the whole can only function when all its myriad parts are allowed to make their contribution without excessive interference by man.

Somehow Christians have to help to establish a sense of trusteeship for the future, and if we do not press for this from a sense of moral obligation, I do not see any politicians bothering their heads. But this respect for nature must also involve a sense of personal moderation. That will not be popular, and it will certainly go against the current social fashion. The Bible, however, does have a lot to say about greed, envy and intemperance. All Christians are encouraged towards self-denial.

You will think all this is hopelessly idealistic and unrealistic. It is certainly idealistic, and no Christian should be ashamed of that. It certainly goes against current trends and attitudes, but Christians have changed attitudes before – over slavery, over prison reform, over treatment of the sick. You may think that the problem is too huge. After all, the people are already born who will double the population of the world in the next thirty years. What can 'little me' do? You will remember that it was just such an attitude that led decent Germans to accept Hitler.

Man has been entrusted with dominion over this world. Christians must press for a responsible, long-term and unselfish interpretation of that trusteeship. If we do not, we shall deny our future, not only for ourselves, but for our children, and, even more important, we shall betray the trust that man has been given by God to have dominion over nature.

'And God said, "Have dominion over every living thing." '

10
Fairness

'JESUS LOOKED AROUND,
GRIEVED AT THE HARDENING OF THEIR HEARTS.'
ST MARK, CHAPTER 3, VERSE 5

I believe that we are witnessing throughout the world a period when human hearts are hardening. In one sense, of course, we see just the opposite – amazing generosity and a deep level of concern for the less fortunate. On the other hand we also see a growing and increasing divide between rich and poor, both individually and by countries; and an appalling escalation of bigotry and intolerance, armed with the weapons of violence and terror.

I suspect that this hardening of heart has come about partly as a result of actions taken by one sector of the community which have led to reactions by other sectors. These in turn lead to a drift towards extremes, both nationally and internationally. The defenders of the middle ground are in retreat, and those who pursue extreme objectives are in the ascendant. Consensus is out, and confrontation is the fashion. And this is true throughout our international society, in politics, in education, in art, and in religion.

The weakness of the middle position – of moderation and of consensus and compromise – is that it seems to be weak and wishy-washy. It gives the appearance that you do not know where you stand. It does not offer an easy, understandable and straightforward solution. The middle of the road is full of 'ifs' and 'buts', of uncertainty, and of being prepared to adapt one's position. This is one reason why people get so angry with the Church of England – 'Why doesn't the Church give a moral lead?' Remember that the Church is there to let its moderation be known unto all men, as St Paul advised the Philippians, and it knows that there is no easy answer. Oh yes, it is easy to generalise. We are all against sin. The difficulty arises when we come down to the particular, and someone asks, 'Is it really wrong if I do this, or take that short cut?' We are all so expert at rationalising our motives that we are able to justify anything.

So in desperation we look for certainty, just because we are not strong enough to live with uncertainty. But certainty so often leads to arrogance: 'I know that I am right!' Religious certainty is perhaps one of the worst forms of arrogance, for it is spiritual and not superficial; it comes from deep within each one of us. Jesus told us that it is what comes from within a man that defiles him. If you are sure that you have a hot line to God, who may then disagree with you? For disagreement becomes then blasphemy against God.

But the real spiritual danger of the extreme position is that it inevitably leads to excess, since excess is the enemy of moderation. Excess led to the Spanish Inquisition, as today it leads to Shiite Muslim terrorism, to hijacking, and in this country to soccer hooliganism. The equivalent danger is that the provocation caused by one excess will lead to the retaliatory action of another; and so the spiral of violence and reaction is started. How difficult it is to halt we can see in the Middle East or in Northern Ireland.

Why have we drifted to extremes? One reason may be the sheer greed that underlies the philosphy of our Western-type affluent society. There is an innate sense in British people of fairness. We really do long to be fair, but too often it is in a negative rather than in a positive way. Because of this we tend to be looking over our shoulders to see what the other person is doing – how he or she is faring. Then envy, which is the bane of English people, always corrupts our desire to see justice done, and shifts the baseline of our judgement from fairness to jealousy. 'He is paid the same as I am and yet he doesn't do as much – that's not fair!' 'He is allowed this or that privilege, which I don't get. That's unfair!'

Although any moderate person will try to ensure as just a balance as is humanly possible, there can never be complete fairness. The more crowded our island becomes, the more difficult it is to allocate scarce resources fairly, and the harder it becomes to achieve complete justice. Indeed, we should probably be happier if only we could realise that it is an unnatural wish to be fair. For nature is not fair. Why should that lovely young mother of thirty develop cancer? Why should that young man of nineteen be killed as a passenger in that car? One of the hardest moral lessons which we have to teach our children is that the world which they are entering is not a fair place.

So often it is our rebellion against injustice that gets carried to extremes, and when envy is fed by excess we become satiated with ambition and discontent. A moderate sense of ambition is a good and healthy thing, but so often today ambition can scarcely be distinguished from jealousy, and that then becomes crippling to the development of our personality. There is the well-known story of the American workman who saw his boss drive by in his Cadillac and said to himself, 'One day I will have a Cadillac.' A fair ambition to improve one's lot. The British workman saw his boss in a Rolls and thought, 'Why should he have that, take it away from him!' Ambition linked to jealousy is always destructive and crippling.

Sometimes jealousy arises from our own sense of inadequacy and insecurity. We see a colleague doing something which we know we ought to be doing, or doing it better than we know we are able to do, and we feel inadequate, shown up and guilty. This sense of inadequacy and guilt has then to be rationalised, so that it may remain tolerable for us to live with our guilt, especially if we are reluctant to do anything about it. And the easiest way out of that sort of situation is envy.

Medieval man personified evil into the person of the Devil, and it was a useful symbol. Evil is still very real and needs to be recognised. The old saying that the road to hell is paved with good intentions is so true. As soon as a good idea or thought appears, the power of evil – the Devil – is there to tempt you to taint it. It is not for nothing that the first temptation was to eat of the fruit of the Tree of Knowledge. For with all the good and the understanding that knowledge brings, within it also hides the Devil. The more we know, the more we question, the more we see the unfairness of our situation, and the more we are tempted to feel frustration or envy.

Perhaps what Jesus is calling us to understand is not so much the world in which we live, as to understand ourselves. And that can be a very painful and demanding task. For when we spend our time looking at others, and wanting to be better or equal to them, we are merely using this as a device to avoid the uncomfortable process of being honest with ourselves. What we do is transfer our problems onto others; it is a very noticeable fact that so often what we say about others actually says much more about ourselves. We tend to reveal our real selves by the way we judge others. Jesus said to the man working on the Sabbath, 'Man, if thou knowest what thou doest, thou art blessed; but if thou knowest not, thou art cursed.' It requires all of God's grace to be honest with oneself, and then to accept one's shortcomings, and still humbly to be able to live at peace with oneself. But that is our vocation, for without that self-awareness we can never improve, and then our hearts do harden, for we have to protect ourselves somehow. And hardness of heart makes us very open to excess of all sorts.

I suppose that the greatest example of unfairness, which we are called upon to follow, lies in Jesus himself. He went about doing good, he cured the sick, gave the blind sight, and challenged men by his refusal to accept automatically the conventions of the time, and by his complete honesty. What was the result? They executed him. We do not like to be challenged. We do not like to have our own inadequacy shown up by the sheer goodness of others. So we can react in one of two ways. We can harden our heart, and be envious – an all too common reaction, which made Jesus look around, grieved at the hardening of their hearts. The other reaction is the one to which you and I are called, as soon as we claim to be Christians. It is to accept your particular cross, and to follow him with the same humility and courage that he showed in spite of all the unfairness of what they did to him.

II

Faith and Hope

'FAITH, HOPE AND CHARITY,
BUT THE GREATEST OF THESE IS CHARITY'

This morning, instead of concentrating upon charity, I want to look at faith and hope. It seems to me that hope these days is at a premium. Until quite recently we believed that science and technology gave us the key to unlimited progress. We thought that things could always be improved, that free democratic institutions would establish themselves all over the world, and that our growing mastery over nature would provide the foundation for an enlightened civilisation that would do away with poverty, hunger, sickness and war. We lived in the belief that things could and would be improved, and that we were steadily moving towards a better future for ourselves and our children.

I see little signs of such confidence today. The sort of hope for the future that was present even forty years ago no longer exists today. For the middle-aged and elderly there is, for the most part, only the hope of a reasonably comfortable old age amid the disintegration of so many old, cherished and familiar values. For the young science and technology are often seen more as a threat than as grounds for hope. The growing attraction of the environmental lobby, the 'Green movement', the anti-this and anti-that movement, are an indication of this shift in perspective from hope and confidence in the future to despair and cynicism. Among the most rapidly growing illnesses are those concerned with mental stability, stress and anxiety, all of which are closely concerned with the collapse of meaning and a sense of purpose. Too many people, young and old, have lost confidence in the validity of our civilisation.

Both Marxism and the liberal capitalism of the West have had as their hope the building of a heavenly city here on earth, the one by evolution, the other by revolution. Our loss of a sense of hope is nowhere more vividly displayed than in the mindless vandalism and thuggery of those who can only express their frustration and envy by smashing the symbols of meaningless affluence, and by the equal folly of the power politics engaged in by the super powers.

The added twist is that our civilisation has extended into every corner of the world, creating a universal culture in the sense that Western competence dominates all races as the vehicle of 'modernity' – with all the implications of technical mastery and powers of discovery, innovation and control that go with it. We Westerners mastered the secret of a scientific method which was true and which banished superstition, and we became the missionaries of light to a dark world. We felt that we had the duty and the means to carry this enlightenment to the whole world. This we have done, with incredible material success but with disastrous moral results. And the reason why this missionary zeal has been so fraught is that the very means by which we have sought to enlighten the world has separated hope from faith.

The Age of Enlightenment seemed to free men's minds from the religious dogmas of the Middle Ages and to offer them a rational explanation which satisfied them as being true – true because it was an appeal to their reason rather than to what seemed then to be their blind credulity. The 'real' world became the world of observable fact. Analysis and objectivity replaced dogma and credulity. Science could accept no authority other than that of observable facts, and so the study of nature – of the Universe – replaced the idea of God. The intellect became supreme, emotion and feelings were not to be trusted. Economics became separated from ethics, and so lost its moral imperative. No wonder that we fail to match our technological skill with the moral ability to use it for man's comfort rather than for his destruction.

Medieval man had the faith that he was not only living for himself but that his work would help to determine the future. He built our beautiful parish churches to the glory of God, with the best art and materials that he could summon. When he used the resources of nature, he was concerned, where possible, to replace them for the future, even though he knew that he personally would never reap the benefit. He was concerned with honour and integrity, whereas modern man has come to think more in terms of himself and his own status. So our thinking has shifted from an emphasis upon duty to an obsession with rights, leading all too often to envy. As our rights could no longer be secured by a religion which seemed to be based upon dogma and superstition, and a sense of man's inadequacy and sinfulness, rather than on his potential, rationality and power, we turned to the State to secure these rights, which now became ours by entitlement. Nationalism replaced God as our effective ideology; no longer were people tried for blasphemy, but instead treason became the most heinous of crimes; no longer the sin against God, but the sin against the State. National governments were now to be responsible for providing freedom from fear, hunger, disease and want – indeed they were to be responsible for the pursuit of happiness, for which earlier generations had looked to God and religion.

We are now the heirs of this scientific world-view. Its method is to identify a problem, analyse its causes, and then seek a solution based upon analyses of the situation. The trouble is that we are becoming increasingly sceptical that an intellectual solution divorced from feeling and morality can supply an answer to our problems, just because every problem has a moral and spiritual aspect. The planting of young oak seedlings to replace those cut down is in itself a parable of faith. For those who plant will not live to see the fruits of their action. They are planting in the hope that this act of faith will be held in trust by those who follow after for the good of future generations.

Our human critical faculty can only operate on the basis of faith. A scientist will proceed with an experiment on the basis of what he believes to be true – he then submits his belief as a hypothesis to critical questioning and experiment. But the questioning is always secondary to what he first believes. Indeed, it is impossible to doubt all one's beliefs; if you do, it is the road to breakdown and mental instability. Isaiah says, 'Unless you believe, you will not understand.' 'Credo ut intelligam,' said Augustine, 'I believe in order that I may understand.' Faith is not an end in itself, the refuge of those who are not prepared to think, as it is sometimes made out to be. Rather it is the starting point from which our thinking and understanding begin.

The trouble is that the Church itself has become unbalanced by the scientific method, and has lost its own faith in the very truth for which it exists. And yet the Church is the only guardian of our one means of understanding ourselves and the world in which we live. If medieval man went too far in terms of credulity, modern man goes to the other extreme in terms of rationality. We have thrown out the baby of faith with the bathwater of credulity. Our most fundamental human beliefs are of the human spirit and they cannot always be demonstrated by the scientific method, and so they have to be held in faith. Convictions that arise from our emotions and from our personal experiences of the human spirit may defy analysis, and yet happiness, grief, peace of mind, freedom, justice and compassion are very real none the less. The Christian clings to the belief that these spiritual experiences are of God, whose son, Jesus Christ, lived like us, suffered as we have to, and died as each one of us will do – but conquered death. It is in that faith that we are given the clue to understanding the meaning of our own life.

Without faith there can be no start to understanding and no meaning to life, and so no hope. Life will then continue to have no meaning, and our civilisation no future, because there lacks this proper balance between faith and reason. For without faith, there can be no hope.

12
The Press

'THAT THY HOLY SPIRIT MAY DIRECT AND RULE OUR HEARTS'

We are faced with many pressures upon traditional Christian values. There are some who would claim that the balance of British society has altered so radically that Christian values can no longer be used as a determining factor. We live in a pluralist age where the majority no longer practise the Christian religion, or have no more than a peripheral belief in it, and where a substantial minority are busy building mosques, Hindu temples, Sikh gadwaras, Buddhist shrines and Rastafarian meeting places. Because the Church of England is a national church, its utterances are often seen as outmoded, and a vain attempt to regain a vanished influence and position in a society that no longer represents these old allegiances. If one accepts that argument, who is to be the guardian of moral values? The public cannot have it both ways; they cannot on the one hand complain that the Church is only concerned with its own internal affairs and never gives a public lead, and then, when someone does have something to say, immediately accuse it of interfering in matters outside its own competence.

In recent months I have become increasingly concerned at the moral values exhibited by certain sections of the national Press. Christians have to question whether or not such a national institution, the Fourth Estate, can continue to command their unqualified support and confidence. Are the considerable liberties which are rightly given in a democratic society to ensure the freedom of the Press being matched by a sense of responsibility equal to the privileges being enjoyed? The problem is one of public values and standards, and it concerns the moral judgements of individuals. Those individuals who are Christians have a right to expect some guidance and support from the Church.

The national Press sets itself up to be a moral judge. The way in which it decides upon what is 'news' constantly involves moral decisions, for there is no such thing as a value-free judgement. Indeed, in many ways the Press could be seen as having replaced the Church as the arbiter of modern values and standards. But this should not absolve Christians from examining whether this moral influence has reached a stage where it corrupts and becomes pernicious. The Holy Spirit is meant to direct and guide our hearts.

If there are moral abuses, it has to be said that they tend to be confined to a small section of the national Press. It is one, however, which still exerts a great deal of influence, and so does open its methods and values to question. There are at least three areas which ought to give the Christian cause for concern.

The first is investigative journalism. When an individual, particularly someone in a position of public trust and responsibility, behaves in a manner that is likely to undermine public confidence, then the Press has a clear duty to report that conduct; that is part of the consequence and the responsibility involved in entering public life. But when large sums of money are paid, often to individuals of questionable moral standing, in order to stimulate a *cause célèbre* which will be sensational and titillate our inborn love of scandal, then both the means and the end deserve to be questioned by those who try to base their values and their lives on the teaching and example of Jesus Christ.

When the Press attacks an individual, that person seems to have everything stacked against him or her. Once the smear has been published, the damage has been done. Any subsequent retraction, even if it be so unusual as to be printed where anyone will notice it, does not undo the harm caused. Complaints to the Press Council seem to be treated almost with scorn by the perpetrators of bad reporting. As Shakespeare had Mark Antony say of Caesar, 'The evil that men do lives after them, the good is oft interrèd with their bones.'

There is no doubt that the Press has exposed many cases of bad conduct, but surely those investigating such cases have a particular responsibility to be sure of their facts, lest an innocent person is publicly tortured. So often the impression is given that if the story is sensational enough, and likely to be of commercial profit to the paper, then the individual does not matter. And yet each one of us is more precious in the sight of God than any other thing.

When innocent men and women go to the courts to clear their names, they have to be rich to succeed against the commercial power of a national newspaper. The legal process is likely to be long drawn out, it will bring enormous pressures on the victim's personal, public and private life, and it will do just what the originators of the smear wanted it to do – it will lead to increased publicity and intrusion. Can the innocent who are so wronged be blamed if they suffer the wrong, and keep their heads down in silence, rather than bring upon their families the strains involved? Surely the time has come when Christians have to say that this state of affairs is unjust. Too often the Press have substituted licence for liberty. These excesses make good people and true think twice about entering public life, and they undermine public confidence in the ability of the courts to protect the ordinary person.

The second area which gives cause for concern is the invasion of personal privacy. It is not only journalists going to undue lengths to extract information or to exploit grief, it is also the manner in which press photographers will go to any length to obtain pictures which are ambiguous or compromising, and which catch the victim unawares. When this is allowed to happen it is all too easy for the public demonstration of bad taste to start to set the norm. For the first time in my experience here at St George's, in the midst of a wedding mini-cameras hidden in ladies' handbags were suddenly produced, and we were subjected to a barrage of flashes. When the culprits were challenged later, the immediate response was: 'The Press do it all the time.'

There are times and places when the individual has the right to privacy, and to deny that right is to bring unfair stress upon personal freedom in the spurious name of a so-called freedom of the Press and public interest, where the Press itself is the sole arbiter of what that interest shall be.

The third matter for concern lies in the distortion and exaggeration of facts, and the way in which they are presented. Two weeks ago a cricket match was reported in some of the Sunday newspapers as having been riven by racist conflict, with the police being called in to separate brawlers. I was there from start to finish, and no such thing ever happened. There were no brawls and the police confirmed that there were no complaints. But because it was in the papers everyone believed it.

We all have these experiences of being involved in or having personal knowledge of an incident, which we then read about in the Press. All too often we say to ourselves, 'But that is not how it happened.' And yet when we read something about someone else, we tend to believe it – because it was in the papers.

The moral issue is whether the Press is purely a commercial concern, free to maximise its sales by any means, or whether it is a public institution which has some moral responsibilities, which should constrain its methods and its standards? One thing is clear: no one can expect to have it both ways, for with freedom goes responsibility.

I believe that this has become a matter which must concern all people of Christian conscience. We all read the newspapers, and so we are all morally concerned as consumers. The freedom of the Press is absolutely vital to a free people, and any constraints upon that freedom would be most unfortunate. But the bad behaviour of the few may build up a public feeling which could result in an increasing call for parliamentary action. Once the long-suffering British public comes to feel that the little man is getting an unfair deal, it will bring political pressure to bear, and that time may not be so far off as the Press would like to imagine.

If we value the freedom of the Press, and wish to see it responsibly preserved, we, as individuals, need to voice our concern whenever we read or see something that we believe to be an abuse of free speech. Freedoms have to be fought for constantly, tyranny and evil only succeed when good people do nothing. So we who are Christians must try to let God's Holy Spirit direct and rule our hearts.

13
Thankfulness

'DO NOT YIELD YOUR MEMBERS TO SIN,
BUT YIELD YOURSELVES TO GOD
AS MEN WHO HAVE BEEN BROUGHT FROM DEATH TO LIFE'
ROMANS, CHAPTER 6, VERSE 13

When I was a boy, the Devon village in which I grew up had no electricity, and most of the villagers drew their water in galvanised buckets from standpipes. Some village children went barefoot, especially in the summer months. Each succeeding generation accepts, as a matter of right, those advantages which their grandparents at their age did not know and were not able to enjoy. It is so easy to forget the progress that has been made, and to take for granted achievements for which we ought to be very thankful.

There is no doubt that material progress has been enormous. I am not so sure that progress in human happiness has been so marked. Are we any more contented, or at peace within ourselves? Has our material advance been matched by that spiritual growth which alone can make it all worthwhile? Are we able to appreciate what we have gained?

Perhaps we have forgotten how to be thankful. Thankfulness is an essential part of good manners, just because gratitude recalls what others have done for us. It turns us away from ourselves – and from selfishness – towards someone or something else. Courtesy is the lubricating oil of life. Hearts, like doors, open with ease to very little keys, and two of these are 'Thank you, sir', and 'If you please'.

Our faith reminds us to be thankful – thankful for things we all too readily take for granted, when we bother to give them any thought at all. Thankful to God for all the possibilities he has opened to us through the life, example, death and Resurrection of Jesus. We forget what all that cost in pain and suffering and unselfishness.

For Jesus showed us that our God is a God of love and happiness. The old law was a law of revenge, of tit for tat, an eye for an eye and a tooth for a tooth. Jesus set us an example of supreme love on the Cross, and even in his agony he was able to pray: 'Father, forgive them.' And God answered his self-effacing obedience by raising him from death, and breaking down that last dread barrier that awaits each one of us. Jesus lived and died in obedience to God, and for other people. God raised him from the dead to show how great is his love for us.

We need to be thankful to a God who cares so deeply, and not only for you and me, but for the whole of his universe. Each sparrow, Jesus told us, is of infinite worth. Perhaps man has become too selfishly absorbed with himself and has forgotten that he is only one small part of God's total creation. The world does not exist for man alone, but man's existence is dependent upon nature, and can only be lived in relation to that nature. We are not helpless in the grip of a malevolent or indifferent fate, ruled by forces beyond our control. Man holds the answer to much of his own future, for good or for ill. We can treat God's creation responsibly and with respect, or fecklessly and with abandon. Sometimes our conduct gives the impression that we are like so many lemmings rushing to our own destruction.

My concern is that so many have become so absorbed with themselves, and with the here and now, that they have forgotten or rejected the experience of the past, and are too busy to be concerned about the future. You know the teenager's prayer: 'God, give me patience, and I want it right *now*!'

Right and wrong seem to have become confused, and the borderlines have become increasingly blurred. We have forgotten the Ten Commandments, or perhaps we treat them like an examination paper, 'Not more than two to be attempted at any one time'! Too many people, even in positions of trust and responsibility, slip into wrong conduct. And yet these will be among the first to pay lip service to the values and standards which they themselves fail to practise. I am reminded of the Calman cartoon, where this little man is saying, 'I'll just carry on with what I am not doing.'

We are brought up in the Christian faith; this is our heritage, for which we all ought to be thankful. But you cannot sustain Christian values of right and wrong without Christian belief, and you cannot maintain any belief worth the name without Christian commitment. Too many pay only lip service to these Christian values, and their actions tell us that all that really matters to them is money, power, status and acquisition.

The editor of the business magazine *Management Today* makes the point about business leadership, when he observes that breaking your word, lying for the sake of lying, blaming others for your own mistakes, is still looked upon in commerce as wrong, *provided that* the making of money is not at stake. But if it is, then these same offences become justifiable, so long as they are practised with discretion. It almost seems as if they are trying to square the circle by convincing themselves that being moral in one way enables them to be less ethical in another, where the making of money is involved.

And yet how refreshing it is to meet someone who says 'I am so lucky, and I have so much for which to be thankful', or 'Please don't be concerned about me, there are so many others so much worse off than I am.' Our personal lives are the best demonstration of our deepest convictions. That is why the Gospel story is so compelling, for Jesus was as human as you and I. He dreaded pain, suffering and loneliness as much as we do. 'My God, my God, why hast thou forsaken me?' 'Oh God, take this cup from me, but not my will but thine be done.' And yet, in spite of this human dread, he was consistent and loyal to what he knew to be right. And that is always what commands respect: people who are consistent, and whose personal example demonstrates their convictions, because they are not ultimately concerned with themselves but with something higher and bigger than themselves.

This is the essence of thankfulness – other people, other ideas, other things. Our faith tells us to be thankful for the means of grace and the hope of glory, that will turn us away from our selfish preoccupations; and not to yield our members to sin but yield ourselves to God, as men who have been brought from death to life.

14
Truth

'I AM THE WAY, THE TRUTH AND THE LIFE'

The Christian has a bounden duty to follow truth, wherever it may lead. But it was Pontius Pilate who asked the question, 'What is truth?'

Modern man has tended to look upon truth as being only those facts which can be logically or scientifically proved. If it works, it is true. If it does not work, then it is not true. There is a great deal of validity in this view. It is the means which has given us a vast and impressive increase of knowledge, and the ability to improve and extend the quality of our lives. But this view of truth is not the whole truth. For as well as enriching human life, the scientific technological view of truth has also threatened and distorted our lives, and even brought us to the edge of disaster. For while the way in which things work may convey one aspect of truth, it does not cover the manner in which this knowledge is put to use. We may have the power and ability to do all manner of things, but do we have the moral will and ethical conviction to use our knowledge for good, rather than for evil?

It is this failure to distinguish between opposites, or rather complementary aspects of truth, that has undermined so much confidence in religious truth. We seem to be addicted to taking far too simplistic a view of life, and for this scientists are as much to blame as theologians. Religious truth, of its very nature, tends to refer to things that cannot be established as physical facts. Indeed, if they could be proved in this way, they would not be religious truths but would fall into the category of the natural sciences. That does not mean to say that they are not true, for truth, as well as being capable of being demonstrated, can also be experienced. You may be able to prove the temperature of your bath water – but you can also experience it. No one can prove by scientific means whether you are happy or sad, but you can certainly feel both of those emotions.

The fact that a religious statement seems to conflict with observed physical phenomena merely proves that man is not just a material observable fact, but that the human spirit is equally vital and is in itself autonomous, and in this sense religious experience is independent of physical data. Religious truth has a certain freedom from scientific truth, because its meaning and significance always has a validity of its own, and is experienced on its own merits. If we consider a recent controversy: some Christians will believe it to be physically true that Jesus was born of a virgin, other Christians will say that this is a physical impossibility. But this is a sterile argument, for there can be no logical solution to such an apparent conflict of opinion. Both attitudes are right, and both are wrong, depending upon the point of view from which you start – the rational or the emotional. The term 'physical' is not the only criterion for truth; there is also 'spiritual' truth, which, by its very nature, cannot, and should not, be explained, proved or tested by physical means, any more than physical truths can be proved by spiritual means.

Religious truth transcends consciousness, and yet because language is the only tool which we humans have to describe things, we are obliged to resort to the impossible task of reducing spiritual experience to statements which are confined to physical language, with all its limitations so far as spiritual experience is concerned. So we construct models and draw pictures, whose language and imagery are from the start inadequate to illustrate fully what we are trying to describe. We only have language, yet language is always inadequate. But having used that inadequate tool, we then fall into the trap of accepting its results literally, and arguing about a picture as though it were a technical drawing, rather than a very inadequate artist's impression.

The fact that we have to use these poor images, and that they are unable because of their inadequacy to stand up to rational criticism, does not mean that they are not true. For we are dealing with spiritual facts, which may confound logic but which logic has not the power to eliminate, based as they are upon an emotional foundation which is unassailable by reason. For when we talk about spiritual truths our feelings are being engaged quite as much as our intellects.

God became man in Jesus Christ. In Jesus the two aspects of truth are intermingled, for he was possessed of a fully human nature as well as a fully divine one. These two natures intermingle so thoroughly that any attempt to separate them mutilates both. This holding together in tension of two opposites may be the nearest our finite human minds can reach towards a better understanding of truth.

Psychologically our very humanity is made up of opposites held together in tension. Striving for perfection is often seen as a male quality, whilst the female inclines by nature towards completeness. Perfectionism on its own always end up in a blind alley without the counterpart of completeness, whilst completeness by itself lacks the rigour of the selective values imposed by the search for perfection.

So with Jesus: if you try to de-mythologise him, to remove all the mystery of his ministry, he merely becomes a misunderstood religious teacher, a Jewish reformer, who fell foul of his own people and the Roman authorities. He becomes no different from Wilberforce, Luther, Mother Theresa or a thousand others. Religion without mystery, a God without transcendence, ceases to be God. But mystery is not the same as fiction; mystery consists of spiritual facts which have been repeated over and over again in human experience, resulting in feelings which may transcend logical explanation, and it is when we deny this side of our human nature that we deny the fullness of our humanity.

It is an interesting fact that the more rational and conscious a person becomes, the more that person also becomes separated from his instinct and emotions, and the more prone to make judgements that may be very logical but which take no account of feeling. For anyone who has served amongst so-called 'primitive' peoples, it is very clear that they possess certain senses and awareness which are progressively blunted the more 'civilised' they become.

If Christ had to hold these opposite sides of his nature in

tension – the human and the divine – then if we are made in the image of God, we can expect to do no less if we are to follow truth wherever it leads. There will be times when we, like Jesus, will cry, 'My God, my God, why hast thou forsaken me?' Because we are both rational and emotional – because we possess both intellectual and moral instincts – we shall, as Christians, inevitably be faced with conflicts of duty. If the very nature of God and of truth is to contain opposites in tension, then we can only expect the same within ourselves. In this sense we are made to be both vessels of conflict and those whose vocation it is to be peacemakers by holding the opposite sides of our nature in creative tension.

For the agnostic it is more comfortable to deny the metaphysical. The Virgin Birth, miracles, the Resurrection are just fairy stories, because they cannot be explained by rational means. But the agnostic does not realise that we humans are seldom able to reach out and grasp a spiritual truth, rather we are possessed by it. After all, why should reason be superior to feeling? If spiritual truth has reality because we have experienced it, and that reality is reinforced by the experience of history and of countless other human beings, why should this carry less weight than a rational judgement?

If the pursuit of truth does involve this balancing of opposites, and if God in Jesus became man, and so involved himself in this apparent contradiction, then God has entrusted to us a high vocation in learning to balance these two sides of our nature. In so recognising this duality, we become more able to hold our emotions and intellect together in a tension which uses the fullness of the power which God has entrusted us to use in a responsible manner.

We shall only make progress in so far as we get to know ourselves and our own nature. And as we are made in the image of God, we shall never understand our complex inner nature until we strive to know God better. For, as Jesus said, 'I am the Way, the Truth and the Life.'

15
Wholeness

The Book of Job opens with the words, 'There lived in the land of Uz a man of blameless and upright life named Job.' All of us who are Christians try to live an upright and blameless life. We may vary in the emphasis which we place on what is upright, but certainly one factor could be summed up in the word 'integrity'. We rightly admire anyone whom we believe to have integrity. And yet what do we mean by that?

The dictionary defines integrity as 'wholeness, soundness, uprightness, honesty'. A man or woman who has integrity is someone then who is a whole person, and yet the same dictionary definition of 'integrated', while it does indeed give 'whole and complete', also says 'made up of parts'. Therefore a lack of integrity results when that wholeness disintegrates or breaks down, and particular parts predominate and get out of balance.

Many of us are like Job. We think that if we behave honestly and uprightly, God will – or at any rate should – reward us. If we believe in a just God – a fair God – then evil ought to be punished and good rewarded. The story of Job tells us that it does not always work this way. The maturity, the integrity, to which Job's sufferings led him, was to a wholeness that was able to accept that God cannot always be judged by purely human standards, and that it is part of man's folly to try to judge God at all. For if man is able to judge God, he puts himself on an equality with God. And then God ceases to be God.

Job's comforters came to sympathise, and to point out to Job the traditional view, that in some way Job could not have been as perfect as he claimed. His sufferings must be due to some evil committed by him, or to some hidden imperfection in him. But Job refuses to accept this line of argument. His refusal upsets his comforters because it challenges their acceptance of the Old

Testament view of a just God. They believed that goodness *is* rewarded, and that sins *are* punished by God. They stood for a sort of moral balance sheet. That put Job into the position, if he accepted their thesis, of having to admit to something he did not believe, that his misfortune was justified. Or he could reject their argument, and then he was rejecting the traditional and accepted religious view of those days.

There was a sense in which Job wanted to confirm the belief in which he had been brought up. He wanted to return to his former prosperity, and to the position where he was still able to believe that his integrity – his wholeness – rested on those traditional beliefs. What a comfort and relief that would have been. It is very disturbing to have everything that you have believed in for years suddenly shattered. When things fall apart, we are no longer at ease, and we feel very insecure. But the experience of his sufferings had convinced Job that those very traditional views were inadequate to explain his situation. It was a case of heads they won, and tails he lost. He was in a double bind.

So often we are quick to condemn what we see as undesirable views, and label the holders as being mentally unbalanced or sick. We need to be very careful how we make such judgements, for this is what the Soviets do in their psychiatric hospitals. If anyone holds views which are contrary to the accepted Marxist norm, then those people must be sick and in need of psychiatric treatment. There are so many Christians who are, or who have been, in mental hospitals within the Soviet system, because by Soviet standards anyone who believes in God must be sick, and therefore in need in psychiatric treatment. This was Job's position; he was challenging the accepted wisdom, and so he must be sick. We need to be very careful before we judge those with whom we disagree. It is an attitude which has led to the Inquisition, to Nazi concentration camps, and now to Islamic Jihad.

Job had begun to realise that, as a mortal man, he was in no position to judge the fairness or wisdom of God. His sufferings had taught him that reward and punishment cannot be related to moral rectitude or to sin in an exact accounting proportion. We may appeal to the justice of God, but we have to do so realising that God cannot be regulated by the moral laws by which we humans seek to rule our earthly lives, even when we believe those laws to be given by God. We are human, and we need laws to guide us in our human frailty, but God is eternal, and we are in no position to judge him by our weakness.

Indeed, if we only do good because we believe that in the end we shall be rewarded, those good acts do not count for much, even in our human judgement. Jesus had plenty to say on that score. The collision between Job's contention that his sufferings were unjust, and his concept of a just and reasonable God, had merely aggravated his sufferings. That line of thought led to a dead end, where a perfect Job was the victim of an unjust and capricious God. The trouble was that Job did not have integrity, in the sense that he was not whole and was not integrated. Like so many of us who strive to live good lives, Job suppressed and was ashamed of other qualities within his personality, just because the society of his time considered them to be bad or suspect.

All of us are victims, like Job, of this unconscious turmoil, for the conflict between the old and accepted norms and emerging new ideas is the generator of anxieties which sometimes are almost too hard to bear. What attitude should parents of my generation adopt when our children and their friends sleep and live together outside marriage? Disapproval can drive them from us; approval is something most of us cannot honestly give. What should a businessman do, when in an African or Middle Eastern country he is expected to bribe, and the jobs of those for whom he is responsible may depend upon his getting that contract? New ways and new ideas are understandably to be feared. The old ways have the safety of familiarity, and acceptance of the new can so often seem to be disloyalty to all that one has been brought up to believe.

But how many of us really want justice? All who aim at perfection, and all who fall short, must then suffer the judgement of their imperfection. And that means all of us all the time. True justice is far too threatening a concept. What we really want – and expect for ourselves – is love and compassion. And if we hope that for ourselves, should we not wish it for others?

If we should not judge others, we certainly cannot judge God. All we can do is to stand in awe of him. If we cannot even control our own destiny or fate, we certainly cannot control God. The story of Job tells us that the old arrangement between God and the Jews – the Covenant of the Chosen People – could never work on a merely contractual basis, as Job in the end was forced to admit. 'I know Thou canst do all things and that no purpose is beyond Thee.'

In front of God, the Supreme Judge, we can only kneel in awe, hoping that the love he showed the world in his son, Jesus Christ, will also be shown to you and me, when we have to answer for the way we have lived our lives. And it is when we reach that state of grace that even when we do not approve of the actions of others, we do not judge them, but have the same compassion and understanding that Jesus showed to the ordinary people of his day; it is then that we begin to be whole. When we can incorporate all those parts of ourselves which we so often deny, those things for which we are ashamed, which we fear, which make us angry – in fact, our humanity, it is then that the perfection which we shall never fully attain on this earth becomes integrity.